How Not to Become a Crotchety Old Man

How NOT to Become a Crotchety Old Man

Mary McHugh

Illustrations by Adrienne Hartman

Andrews McMeel
PUBLISHING®

Andrews McMeel Publishing
a division of Andrews McMeel Universal
1130 Walnut Street, Kansas City, Missouri 64106

www.andrewsmcmeel.com

18 19 20 21 22 WKT 19 18 17 16 15

ISBN: 978-0-7407-3952-1

Library of Congress Control Number: 2003062817

Book design by Holly Ogden

Attention: Schools and Businesses

Andrews McMeel books are available at quantity discounts with bulk purchase for educational, business, or sales promotional use. For information, please e-mail the Andrews McMeel Publishing Special Sales Department: specialsales@amuniversal.com.

Introduction

Crotchety Old Men are everywhere: on the road crouched behind the wheels of old gas guzzlers; at home whining because they can't find their glasses, keys, or wallets; stomping around grocery stores grumbling that they don't sell any decent food anymore; and bent over their morning newspapers foaming at the mouth at the most recent outrages committed by politicians.

We all have Crotchety Old Men in our lives. Your Crotchety Old Man could be your father, your grandfather, your older brother, your husband, or even—*you!* Crotchety

Old Men can easily be identified by remarks such as "What's this white stuff all over my meat?" and "If they don't stop sending money to all those foreign places, this country will be bankrupt in five years!" If you even suspect you might be one or if you're sure that you're living with one, you will recognize the following signs.

Crotchety Old Men . . .

Should never wear Speedos.

Consider Anna Nicole Smith
the perfect wife.

Don't like to eat
"stuff covered with white sauce."

Actually like prunes.

Think women were born to clean—
like their mothers.

Turn into helpless invalids
when they have a cold.

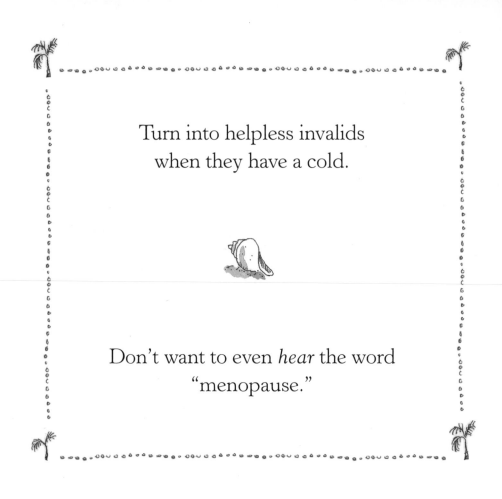

Don't want to even *hear* the word
"menopause."

Love cordless drills as gifts—
no one knows why.

Believe "You look okay" is a compliment.

Wish women would just shut up
and let them talk.

Forget what foreplay means,
if they ever knew.

Think women were invented to look pretty
and have children.

Think their wives should wake up
when they get up in the middle of the night.

Never learned to put a new roll of toilet paper
on the rod.

Think Nixon was a victim of "the media."

Wish somebody would do something about Hillary Clinton.

Don't understand the big problem
with racial profiling.

Believe women aren't smart enough to be
lawyers, doctors, or investment brokers.

Think everybody else should get off the road when they're driving.

Think we should ship all immigrants
back where they came from.

Become couch potatoes
during football season.

Believe cooking is women's work.

Think throwing a steak on the grill is cooking.

Wear plaid pants and green jackets.

A man decided to give his father a ninetieth birthday to remember. He took him out for a spectacular meal in the best restaurant in town, bought tickets for the best play on Broadway, and took him to the Plaza and got him a magnificent suite overlooking the park. He left, knowing there was one more surprise waiting for his father. The old man was getting ready for bed when there was a knock on the door. When he answered it, he saw a gorgeous woman standing there. She purred, "Hi honey, want some super sex?" The old man thought for a minute and then said, "I think I'll just have the soup."

Think somebody else, preferably a woman, should do all the chopping, peeling, seeding, and cleaning up when they make spaghetti sauce.

Believe they were born to be waited on.

Don't know how to take things out of the
dishwasher and put them away.

Grumble that no one looks like them,
sounds like them, eats like them,
or behaves properly anymore.

Still laugh at Abbott and Costello.

Think the clothes they throw on the floor just magically end up in the hamper.

Never read instructions.

Believe lightbulbs burn out much sooner
than they used to.

Are sure their wives spend money
just to annoy them.

Think money should be spent only on beer, golf, and baseball games.

Truly believe women thought up crying just to get their own way.

Never get through a day without asking
at least once, "Where's my . . .
(glasses, keys, papers, etc.)?"

Consider the silent treatment
from their wives a reward.

Think "weekend" means "sports."

Believe mothers-in-law were invented just
to make them miserable.

Do not consider a fart successful unless it is loud.

Look upon belching as an art form.

Think "sensitive man" means "wimp."

Love to explain things you've known
for years.

Believe they haven't gained weight because their belts under their paunches are the same size they were forty years ago.

Exercise only when the batteries in the TV remote control are dead and they have to get up to change channels.

Forget anniversaries and birthdays but remember their golf score the day they broke 100.

Don't understand why doctors can't figure out why their back hurts.

Can't remember how old their
grandchildren are.

Like guns even better than naps.

Consider white wine a sissy drink.

Think most people are stupid.

Think only sissies say "I love you."

Wish John Wayne would come back.

Announce at dinner parties that a woman's place is in the house, not the House.

Wish women would be banned from golf courses and should have separate entrances into country club dining rooms.

Suspect that anyone with facial hair is a terrorist.

Think a good way to start a conversation is
"What did you do in World War II?"

Prefer women who agree with
everything they say.

Never let a day go by without complaining about *something*.

Expect women in their offices—
and homes—to make the coffee.

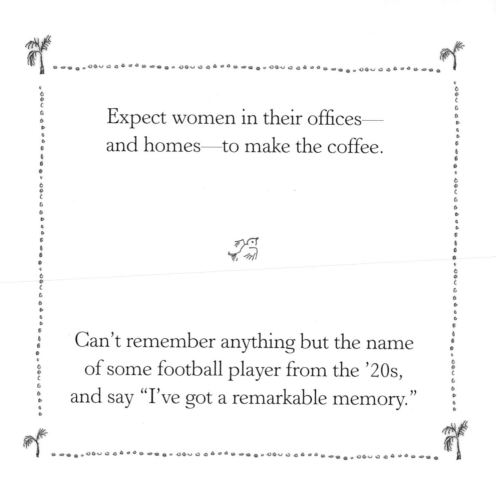

Can't remember anything but the name
of some football player from the '20s,
and say "I've got a remarkable memory."

Still act the way they did in high school.

The difference between men and government bonds is that bonds will mature.

A woman was married to a Crotchety Old Man who always said to her, "When I die, I want you to bury all my money with me. Promise me that." She promised and when the man finally died, a friend asked if she kept her promise. "Oh yes," she said. "I wrote him a check."

Haven't been awake to see in
the New Year since 1948.

Still think a long-distance phone call is
wildly extravagant.

Think if they scramble an egg for
themselves they should be given a medal.

Refer to anyone who has an opinion different from theirs as a "commie-pinko simp."

Won't turn their hearing aid on because "there's too much noise in here!"

Don't understand the concept that if you put something back where you found it, it will be there when you look for it the next time.

Hate every present you give them.

Stand in the middle of the kitchen and say,
"Where's the butter?"

Think Mother's Day and Valentine's Day are fake holidays to get people to spend money.

Consider the words "male chauvinist pig" a compliment.

Remember when a home cost $13,000, and brag about how much their house is worth now, sixty years later.

Wear long underwear in the summer.

Remember when you could replace parts in appliances, and refuse to buy new ones.

Think there hasn't been a great baseball player since Joe DiMaggio, and that includes Mickey Mantle.

Think movies are a total waste of money.

Think there hasn't been a good war
since WWII.

Think they should be praised loudly when they do a load of wash.

Say things like "Kids today have it too easy."

Say things like "Nobody knows how to make a decent pot roast anymore."

Think vegetarians are nut cases.

Don't think there has been a good comedian
since Jack Benny.

An old woman loses both ears in an accident. The plastic surgeon says he will attempt an ear transplant, but the only ears available are a man's ears. She has the surgery, all seems fine, and she goes home. But the next day she calls the doctor in a rage. "You should never have given me a man's ears!" she screams. "Why not?" the surgeon asks. "An ear is an ear. Can't you hear?" "I hear everything just fine," she says. "But I can't understand anything I'm told."

Think the last beautiful movie star
was Sophia Loren.

Are convinced that people who want to save the
whales belong in the loony bin.

Hope everyone at a peace demonstration
will be arrested.

Think men who cry should get over it.

Fall asleep at parties.

Tell long, boring stories with themselves
as the heroes.

Don't understand why everyone
doesn't agree with them.

Hate small talk and think most talk *is* small.

Think when they forget something, it's normal,
but when their wives forget something,
it's Alzheimer's.

Lose their sense of taste as they get older and blame it on their wives' cooking.

Keep saying "Speak up! Don't mumble!"

Only accept the news as reported by the *Wall Street Journal*.

Think the proper present for a wife is another bathrobe.

Consider hardware stores the only stores
worth shopping in.

Talk when you're talking.

Grow hair everywhere but on their heads.

Stomp instead of walk.

Love to say "You don't know what you're talking about."

Don't think anybody can tell they have combed their hair over their bald heads.

Still give advice to their grown children.

Take it personally when the
Dow Jones Industrial Average goes down.

Don't understand African-American names
and think they should all be called
Mary or John.

Won't travel to other countries because
"I haven't seen all of America yet."

Have permanent frown lines.

Start off each day with a complaint about the weather, the news, the neighbors, breakfast, everything.

Remember when you took a job with a company out of college and stayed with them until you were sixty-five and then retired and moved to Florida.

Accuse their wives of shrinking their pants
in the wash.

Say "Whatever happened to Betty Grable?
She had great legs."

Don't see anything wrong with calling
a woman "a broad."

Love dumb-blonde jokes.

Walk in the middle of the sidewalk and expect everyone to get out of the way.

Leave the room when women talk about
their pregnancies or menopause.

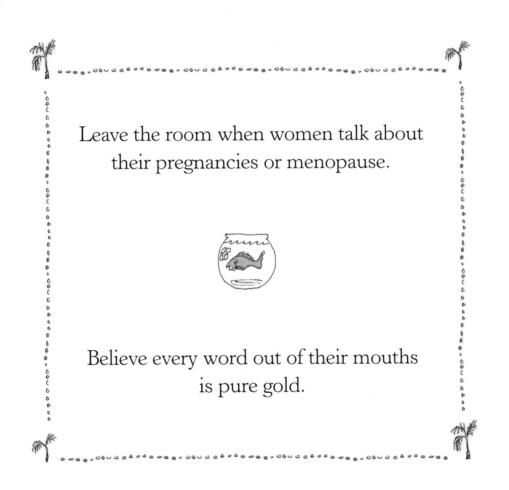

Believe every word out of their mouths
is pure gold.

Hate twenty-four-hour-a-day news channels.
"Twice a day is enough."

Love Rush Limbaugh. Hate Tom Brokaw.

Have no idea
who half the people on *Charlie Rose* are.

Do not understand Adam Sandler at *all*.

An old lady lay in bed dying. She told her husband to bring her a shoebox from the top shelf of her closet. Opening it, he found two doilies and $82,500 in cash. "My mother gave me that box the day we were married," she said. "She told me to make a doily every time I got mad at you." The old man was very touched that in fifty years she'd only been mad at him twice. "Where did the $82,500 come from?" he asked. "Oh," she said, "that's the money I made selling all the doilies I made."

Drink *real* coffee and then stay awake all night.

Can't communicate with their teenaged grandchildren and think it's the children's fault.

Don't understand people who don't eat butter, cream, and eggs.

Think SUVs should be banned from the road.

Turn into giant babies when they
cut themselves.

Love Polish jokes and don't understand why
no one tells them anymore.

Think telling other people what to do
is their birthright.

Refuse to open the windows in winter because "You're heating the whole outdoors."

Think air conditioning gives you colds.

Only read books about presidents and wars.

Don't like novels unless they are by Tom Clancy.

Think all New Age stuff is one more sign
the world is going to hell.

Consider golf the perfect game because
"There are no women allowed in our club."

Say "Where did you hide my socks?"

Think complimenting their wives will spoil them.

Still think Jane Fonda is a traitor.

Think it's their God-given right to drive slowly in the left lane.

Fall asleep in their chair after lunch, before dinner, and after dinner and wonder why they can't get to sleep at night.

Look upon Home Depot as a place of worship.

Wish fedoras and Panama hats would come back.

Are up by 6 A.M. and expect the rest of the
world to be up, too.

Distrust optimists.

Think everybody's nice until
you get to know them.

Don't mind dogs but expect their wives to walk them.

Eat apple pie with a big hunk of rat cheese.

Think the funniest scene in any movie *ever* is the farting scene in *Blazing Saddles*.

Have never forgiven their wives for dragging them to see *Cats*.

Do not approve of female cops, firemen,
or soldiers and barely put up with
women doctors and lawyers.

Hate the French—but then, who doesn't?

Always sound as if they're mad
at something even when they aren't.

Think everyone in this country should speak English.

Still think the Germans are a warlike people. "It's in their blood."

Don't really trust the Japanese because of
Pearl Harbor.

Think only gay people have AIDS.

Tend to growl when they speak.

Do not understand *Seinfeld*.
"Who *are* these people?"

Take mealtimes *very* seriously.

Salt everything automatically
before tasting it.

Accept their own paunches but think their wives should exercise to get rid of their tummies.

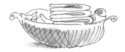

Can't quite believe Tiger Woods.

Need someone to fold their shirts
when they go on vacation.

Think Eminem is a candy.

Yell at anchormen and -women
on newscasts.

Cheat at Scrabble by turning over letters
to make them blanks.

Pretend they read *Playboy* for the articles.

Don't mind being a grandfather so much,
but they hate being married
to a grandmother.

Can only remember the accusative voice
from English class.

Like babies—
when they are in another room.

Think it's funny to ask little kids
"How's your childhood going?"

Go ballistic when a woman uses the men's room
when there's no one in there and there's a
long line for the women's toilet.

Always read the obituary page first
to make sure they're not in there.

Think food is supposed to be meat and
potatoes, not salads.

Never, ever sing in the rain.

Never understood that women don't like
to be called "dearie," as in "That too
complicated for you, dearie?"

Don't understand what's wrong
with hunting.

Think wrestling is a legitimate sport.

Really believe that God made them smarter
than everybody else.

Think they deserve a medal
for taking out the trash.

Think the perfect death would be in the middle of a golf game with their cleats on.

A Crotchety Old Man decided to wash his sweatshirt. He threw it in the washing machine and yelled to his wife, "What setting do I use?" "What does it say on the shirt?" his wife asked. He yelled back, "University of Texas."

Think the way to solve international problems
is to bomb the hell out of them.

Remember when gas cost ten cents a gallon
and tell you about it every time they
fill up their tanks.

Expect somebody else to answer the phone.

A man was visiting an old friend and he was really impressed at the fact that his friend called his wife "honey," "sweetheart," and "darling" every time he spoke to her. The man said, "I think it's wonderful that you call your wife such loving names after all these years of marriage. "Oh," said the friend, "I forgot her name ten years ago."

Think young girls don't wear enough
clothes these days.

Go to doctors as a hobby.

Blame everyone but themselves
when things go wrong.

Wear orange on St. Patrick's Day as a protest.

Can have lunch with an old friend and
not ask "How's your wife?" Or "What are
your children doing now?"

Have mouths that have turned down
at the corners for so long you can't tell
when they're smiling.

Consider that global warming is nonsense thought up by the "touchy-feelies."

A Crotchety Old Man told his wife he would dig himself out of his grave and come back to haunt her if she didn't live a quiet, sober live after he died. "I'll claw my way back up and torment you," he said. After he died, she went out dancing and drinking and laughing every night. "Aren't you afraid your husband will dig himself out of his grave and come back to haunt you?" a friend asked. "Oh, no," the wife said. "Let him dig. I buried him upside down."

Think homeless people are just lazy and could be off the streets if they really tried.

Have earned every frown line on their face.

Think "Casual Fridays" is proof that the business world has lost its mind.

Like any color as long as it's green.

Take it personally if people don't return their calls *immediately.*

Watch sexy ladies exercising on TV and change the channel when someone comes in the room.

Say "The world has gone to hell
in a handbasket."

Cheat on their diets but yell at their wives when they eat one M&M.

Can't tell the difference if you serve margarine instead of butter.

Laugh at their own jokes.

Don't laugh at anyone else's jokes.

Have no clue what to do with leftover food.

If he were still in kindergarten, the teacher
would send a note home to his parents
that said "Does not play well with others."

Think "pigs in a blanket" is not only the
best hors d'oeuvre, but would make
a great dinner.

Collect odd things like bottle-cap openers,
bottle caps, handmade nails, and
miniature screw drivers.

Hum while they eat (like Billy Bob Thornton).

Leave their keys in the bird feeder,
the space heater, and the refrigerator.

Put glue on squeaky door hinges
instead of oil by mistake.

Buy ladybugs to kill the Japanese beetles and
then accidentally open the box in the house.

Disappear into the garage for "spring cleaning" and don't come out until fall.

Hibernate in the winter.

Truly believe there is a logical reason
for everything.

Can cure anyone's insomnia by talking about bird watching, stamp collecting, or baseball statistics.

Get shorter but refuse to admit it.

Start to wear leather jackets,
cowboy boots, and pony tails on
their seventieth birthdays.

Drop jelly beans all over the rug
no matter how many times you tell them
they make the dog sick.

Approve only of dogs as pets (but when no one is looking they'll pat the cat).

Always miss a little patch on the neck
when they shave.

Think they look great in caps.

Buy cans of broken cashews
because they're cheaper.

Threaten to throw the computer
in the trash every day.

Say spiders are good luck so they won't have to kill them.

Refuse to go anywhere
during football season.

Still ask "What kind of name is that?"

Don't understand why they have to put the toilet seat down.

Think tofu would make good grouting.

Will never believe one line in this book
is about them.